Nelson

GRAMMAR

PUPIL BOOK 2

WENDY WREN

Nelson

Book 2 – Contents

This symbol shows that you need to correct mistakes in the text.

Proper nouns

The names of people are special nouns.
Special nouns are called **proper nouns**.

Mrs Peters

Omar

Lorna

The names of places are also proper nouns.

Proper nouns start with capital letters.

Seal Island

River Lee

Midtown

Blake Mountain

GRAMMAR *Focus*

Copy the sentences below into your book.
Write the **proper nouns** with capital letters.

1 A small town called greenwood is near the river mead.

2 The shops are in east street and the bus station is in king street.

3 The town of greenwood is 40 kilometres from leeds.

Look at the words in the box.
Find the names of places.
Copy them and give each one a capital letter.

africa	town	belfast	wales
india	country	city	village
france	rome	scotland	river

GRAMMAR *Extension*

A Copy the sentences below.
Use a **proper noun** to fill each gap.

1 I live in _____.

2 The road I live in is called _____.

3 I would like to visit _____.

4 _____ is the name of a town.

5 _____ is the name of a country.

B Now write your name and address.

Don't forget the
capital letters!

UNIT 2
Adjectives

Adjectives are describing words.
They tell us more about a person or thing.

Colours and numbers can be adjectives as well.

enormous elephant   **old** car

We can also use adjectives to describe the difference between two things.

big bottle   **bigger** bottle   **small** bicycle   **smaller** bicycle

Words like 'bigger' and 'smaller' are called **comparative adjectives**.

GRAMMAR *Focus*

Copy the sentences below into your book.
Add *er* to the end of each **adjective**.

1 This hill is (high) than that one.
2 My hands are (clean) than yours.
3 My radio is (loud) than yours.
4 This bread is (fresh) than those rolls.
5 It is (cold) today than it was yesterday.
6 Is the river (deep) than the pond?

faster

higher

warmer

harder

Copy the sentences below.
Fill each gap with a **comparative adjective** from the box.

1 I can jump _____ than you.

2 This new car goes _____ than our old one.

3 It was _____ to cycle up the hill than it was to cycle down.

4 When the weather gets _____ than it has been lately, you can wear shorts.

GRAMMAR *Extension*

Comparative adjectives compare things.

A Copy the words from the box.
Underline all the **comparative adjectives**.

cold	straight	thicker	softer
sharp	smooth	colder	straighter
great	thick	greater	soft
small	smoother	sharper	smaller

B Use these **comparative adjectives** in sentences of your own.

1 weaker 2 shorter 3 damper

4 darker 5 lower 6 tighter

7

Confusing words

'Two' written as a number is 2.

It is easy to mix up the words **two**, **to** and **too**.

We use **two** as a number:
   In **two** days it will be my birthday.

We use **to** like this:
   I am going **to** the park.

To is also part of a verb family name, like:
   to play   **to** fall   **to** eat

We use **too** to mean 'as well'.
   I am having a cake **too**.
   We had some presents **too**.

Too can also mean that we can't do something:
   This hill is **too** hard for me to climb.
   These books are **too** heavy for me to carry.

GRAMMAR *Focus*

Copy the sentences below into your book.
Fill each gap with *two* or *too*.

1 Please find _____ pencils for me.

2 I have _____ letters to post.

3 It is _____ far to walk to the shops.

4 It is _____ late to go out.

5 I would like an ice lolly _____.

6 If we go to the shop, my sister wants to come _____.

8

Practice

Copy these sentences.
Fill each gap with *to* or *too*.

1 I want _____ play the piano.

2 I would like to play the piano _____ .

3 Do you think it will be _____ hard to learn?

4 You can learn if you really want _____ .

Extension

A Copy these sentences.
Fill the gaps with *two*, *to* and *too*.

1 The _____ times table is easy.

2 I am going _____ a party today.

3 I am _____ tired _____ stay up late.

4 If you get _____ many wrong you will have _____ learn it again.

5 I made _____ mistakes.

B This sentence uses the words **two**, **to** and **too**:

The **two** dogs ran **to** the tree but it was **too** hard to climb.

Now make up your own sentence using *two*, *to* and *too*.

9

Conjunctions

Conjunctions are words we use to join sentences.

The conjunctions **and** and **but** are often used to join sentences.

> I like chocolate cake **and** I ate a large slice.

> I like chocolate cake **but** was I too full to eat any more.

Two other useful conjunctions are **because** and **so**.

Conjunctions stick sentences together.

I don't eat liver. I don't like it.
I don't eat liver **because** I don't like it.

Put the chairs on the table. I can sweep the floor.
Put the chairs on the table **so** I can sweep the floor.

GRAMMAR *Focus*

Use *because* or *so* to join each pair of sentences to make one sentence. Write the sentences in your book.

1 Take a coat. It might rain later.

2 I climbed the tree. I could see over the roof.

3 The lion prowls around. It is hungry.

4 Close the gate. The dog will not get out.

Remember,
pronouns are: I, he,
she, it, we, they.

A Copy the sentences.
Change the brown words into **pronouns**.

1 My brother and I woke up early.
My brother and I heard a bird singing.

2 The football fans cheered.
The football fans saw their team score a goal.

3 Liam lost the key. Liam could not unlock the door.

B Join each pair of sentences that you have made with *because* or *so*.

GRAMMAR *Extension*

and	so
but	because

Use a **conjunction** from the box to complete each of these sentences.

1 Find a cloth ____ wipe the table.

2 Jackie bought some flowers ____ she could use her new vase.

3 I want to go home ____ it is time to eat.

4 The door was locked ____ the window was open.

Verbs

Verbs are doing or active words.

When we use verbs to tell us about something that is happening now, we use the **present tense**.

'Tense' means 'time'.

The car speeds down the street.
The traffic lights change to red.

GRAMMAR Focus

A Copy the sentences below into your book. Underline the **present tense verbs**.

1 I ride my bike.

2 The chain squeaks.

3 The pedals stop.

4 I push my bike.

B Use a **present tense verb** from the box to finish each sentence.

chimes

walks

live

checks

1 Kirsty _____ to school.

2 The teacher _____ the homework.

3 The clock _____ every hour.

4 Rabbits _____ in holes.

Copy the sentences below.
Change each verb family name to a **present tense verb**.

1 The train (to pull) into the station.

2 The people (to get) off when it has stopped.

3 They (to meet) their friends.

4 The train (to leave) the station.

GRAMMAR *Extension*

A Copy the table.
Fill in the missing words.

Family name	Present tense
to know	I _____ he _____
to _____	we climb she _____
_____ give	it _____ they give
to sleep	you _____ she _____

B 1 Choose three **verb family names** from the table and use them in sentences of your own.

2 Choose three **present tense verbs** from the table and use them in sentences of your own.

13

Verbs

Verb family names begin with 'to'.

to swim **to** fly **to** cook

A very special verb family is called the verb 'to be', but it doesn't have the word 'be' in it!

Verbs can be **singular** or **plural**.

This is the present tense of the verb 'to be':

'Singular' means 'one'.
'Plural' means 'more than one'.

Singular	Plural
I am	we are
you are	you are
he is	they are
she is	
it is	

GRAMMAR *Focus*

Copy the sentences below into your book.
Fill each gap with the correct part of the **verb 'to be'**.

1 I _____ two centimetres taller than my brother.

2 You _____ the youngest in the family.

3 He _____ called Jake.

4 We _____ taking the dog for a walk.

5 They _____ my brothers and sisters.

Copy the sentences below.
Choose the right word to finish each sentence.

1 The girl is/are very quiet.

2 The children is/are very naughty.

3 I is/am asleep by nine o'clock.

4 We am/are in the school choir.

5 You are/is the best footballer in the team.

GRAMMAR *Extension*

A Match the words on the left with the words on the right to make sentences.

You	is the only boy.
I	are in the shop.
He	are very late for school.
They	am very tired.

B Find the mistake in each sentence.
Write each sentence correctly.

1 We am farmers.

2 You is a police officer.

3 They is vets.

4 I are a doctor.

Proper nouns

The names of people and places are **proper nouns**.
Proper nouns have capital letters.

Fatima

Sankha

United
Kingdom

Days of the week and months of the year are also proper nouns.

Wednesday   Saturday   February

GRAMMAR *Focus*

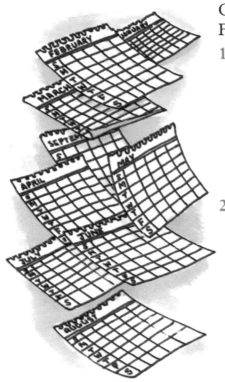

Copy the words below into your book.
Finish each word by adding a **capital letter**.

1 Days of the week:

_unday   _onday   _uesday

_ednesday   _hursday   _riday

_aturday

2 Months of the year:

_anuary   _ebruary   _arch

_pril   _ay   _une

_uly   _ugust   _eptember

_ctober   _ovember   _ecember

Copy the sentences below.
Use a day of the week or a month of the year to fill each gap.

1 _____ is the first month of the year.

2 _____ is the last month of the year.

3 _____ comes after Monday.

4 _____ and _____ are called the weekend.

5 _____ is the third month of the year.

6 _____ is the middle of the week.

GRAMMAR *Extension*

> Special days like festivals are also **proper nouns**:
> Christmas   New Year's Eve   Ramadan

Copy these sentences.
Use capital letters for the **proper nouns**.

1 christmas day is on 25th december.

2 The 1st of january is new year's day.

3 st david's day is an important day in wales.

4 The festival of hanukkah is in december.

Check-up 1

Proper nouns

Copy these sentences into your book.
Write the **proper nouns** with capital letters.

1 I am going sailing on the river dee on tuesday.

2 The bus only goes to bangor on saturday.

3 We are going to america in july.

Adjectives

Copy and complete the **comparative adjectives** in this table.

This torch is bright.	That torch is _____ .
This coat is old.	That coat is _____ .
This road is long.	That road is _____ .
This man is strong.	That man is _____ .
This bag is light.	That bag is _____ .

Confusing words

Copy the sentences below.
Choose the right word to finish each sentence.

1 It is to/too late to go out.

2 I have got too/two minutes too/to catch the bus.

3 Can I come to/too?

4 The dog likes to/two bury his bone.

Conjunctions

Join each pair of sentences with a **conjunction**.

1 I hurt my hand. I cannot write.
2 The girls played very well. They won the netball match.
3 I did not feel well. I had a headache.
4 Alex was late. He missed the bus.

Verbs

A Copy the sentences below.
Change each verb family name to a **present tense verb**.

1 The tree (to grow) near the river.
2 People (to visit) the castle.
3 The owl (to hunt) at night.
4 He (to eat) cereal for breakfast.
5 She (to read) her book in bed.

B Copy the sentences below.
Choose the right word to finish each sentence.

1 The boys am/are on bicycles.
2 Some people is/are fond of animals.
3 Our cat am/is lost.
4 My brother and I is/are in the team.

19

Verbs

The **present tense** of a verb tells you about something that is happening now.

The dog **barks**.

The girl **runs**.

This present tense tells you about an action that is still going on.

Sometimes we need more than one verb to make a sentence work.

Another way to make the present tense is like this:

verb 'to be'	+ verb	+ ing	
I am	+ eat	+ ing	= I am eating.
You are	+ walk	+ ing	= You are walking.
He is	+ look	+ ing	= He is looking.
She is	+ draw	+ ing	= She is drawing.
It is	+ bark	+ ing	= It is barking.
We are	+ talk	+ ing	= We are talking.
You are	+ stand	+ ing	= You are standing.
They are	+ cry	+ ing	= They are crying.

The verb 'to be' is a helper verb.

GRAMMAR *Focus*

Copy the sentences below into your book.
Underline the two words in each sentence that make up the **present tense verb**.

1 The blackbirds are building a nest.

2 The cow is eating the grass.

3 I am walking to school.

4 The gate is swinging in the wind.

5 The boy is kicking a stone.

GRAMMAR *Practice*

Use the helper verb 'to be' and an 'ing' word.

Copy these sentences.
Replace each verb family name with the **present tense verb**.

1 Ann (to lick) her ice cream.

2 The mouse (to sniff) the cheese.

3 We (to play) in the park.

4 I (to read) my comic.

GRAMMAR *Extension*

Watch your spelling! You need to knock off the 'e' at the end of a word before adding 'ing'.

A Copy the table.
Fill in the missing words.

Verb family name	Present tense
to watch	he is _____
_____ buy	we are _____
to wake	you are _____
_____ _____	They _____ striking
to look	it _____ _____
_____ fall	I _____ _____

B Add *ing* to each of these words.

1 wish 2 hit 3 run 4 like

5 put 6 grow 7 start 8 shine

Watch your spelling!

C Add each of the words you made in part B to the verb 'to be' to make sentences of your own.

21

Adjectives

We can use **adjectives** to describe the difference between two things.

'Taller' is a comparative adjective.

a tall tower   a **taller** tower

We can also use adjectives to describe the difference between three or more things.

small flower   smaller flower   **smallest** flower

'Smallest' is a **superlative adjective**.
We add 'est' to the end of the adjective when we compare three or more things.

GRAMMAR *Focus*

Copy these sentences into your book.
Add *est* to each **adjective**.

1. The building is the (high) in town.

2. That is the (bright) star in the sky.

3. Kim is the (young) girl in the class.

4. This is the (strong) rope we sell.

5. Tuesday was the (cold) day this week.

6. This is the (thick) rug in the house.

saddest

darkest

longest

Copy the sentences below.
Fill each gap with a **superlative adjective** from the box on the left.

1 The sky was cloudy and it was the ____ night for a week.

2 We climbed the ____ mountain of the three.

3 I cried because it was the ____ story I have ever read.

GRAMMAR *Extension*

A Copy the table below. Fill in the missing words.

Adjective	Comparative	Superlative
tall	taller	tallest
quick		
soft		
smooth		
warm		
light		

Superlative adjectives compare three or more things.

B Use these **superlative adjectives** in sentences of your own.

1 plainest 2 dullest 3 largest

4 lowest 5 wettest 6 sharpest

Contractions

If something contracts it gets smaller.
Contractions are words that have been made smaller by missing out letters.

An apostrophe like this **'** goes in place of the missing letter or letters.

I am looking for my gloves.
I'm looking for my gloves.

I am	=	I'm	**a** is missed out
you are	=	you're	**a** is missed out
he is	=	he's	**i** is missed out
she is	=	she's	**i** is missed out
it is	=	it's	**i** is missed out
we are	=	we're	**a** is missed out
they are	=	they're	**a** is missed out

GRAMMAR *Focus*

Copy these two lists into your book.
Draw lines to join each word in the first box with the correct **contraction** in the other box.

we are	he's
you are	they're
he is	she's
it is	we're
they are	it's
she is	you're

A Write out the words from which these
contractions are made.

1 she'll   2 they're   3 we're

4 it's   5 you're   6 I'm

B Copy the sentences below.
Make the coloured words into **contractions** by
missing out a letter and using an apostrophe.

1 I am not happy about this.

2 If she is late she will miss the bus.

3 They are going to meet the train.

4 When you are at the shops you
can buy a newspaper.

5 It is colder than it was yesterday.

Match the words with **contractions** from the box.
Write the contractions in your book.

Put the apostrophe
in the space, not
above a letter.

1 I will
2 we are
3 can not
4 I have
5 she had
6 do not
7 would not
8 it will
9 did not
10 who is

I've		it'll
	didn't	
she'd		I'll
who's		wouldn't
can't	don't	we're

25

Adverbs

Adverbs **add** to **verbs**.

An **adverb** tells us more about how, when or where the action of a verb takes place.

The boy is shouting loudly.

The adverb 'loudly' tells us **how** the boy is shouting.

Mrs Green must go today.

The adverb 'today' tells us **when** Mrs Green must go.

I have put the books here.

The adverb 'here' tells us **where** the books have been put.

GRAMMAR Focus

Write in your book a list of the **adverbs** used in these sentences.

1 We put the cat outside when it is dark.

2 Sam carefully copied the sentences.

3 She always buys flowers in the market.

4 It rained heavily all day.

5 I get up early on a Saturday.

Write these headings in your book:

how	when	where

All the words in the box below are **adverbs**.
Put each adverb under the correct heading.

> slowly   later   outside
>
> here   angrily
>
> never   sweetly   neatly

GRAMMAR *Extension*

A Finish these sentences with **adverbs** of your own.

1 The boy sang _____ .

2 The boy shouted _____ .

3 The boy ran _____ .

4 The boy waved _____ .

5 The boy slept _____ .

B Use **adverbs** to write answers to the following questions.

1 When will you do your homework?

2 How do you travel to school?

3 Where do you go shopping?

4 When can you come out to play?

5 How do you clean your teeth?

6 Where do you catch the bus?

27

Prepositions

Prepositions tell us where something is.

Prepositions often tell us about the **position** of something.

The cat is **on** the roof.

I had lunch **after** the football match.

Focus

Copy these sentences into your book.
Choose the right **preposition** from the box to finish each sentence.

through

behind

between

in

near

1 The water is ____ the pan.

2 The house is ____ the trees.

3 The snake is ____ the rock.

4 The shed is ____ the fence.

5 The path goes ____ the wood.

Practice

Look carefully at the picture.
Write some sentences, using **prepositions**, to describe where things are in the picture.

Extension

A Copy and complete these sentences by choosing the correct **prepositions**.

1 I am very angry *for/with* you.

2 The medicine is good *for/of* you.

3 I know I can rely *in/on* you.

B Use these **prepositions** in sentences of your own.

1 *without* 2 *after* 3 *before*

4 *around* 5 *between* 6 *at*

Articles

The vowels are:
a, e, i, o and u.
The other letters
are consonants.

The words 'a' and 'an' are called **articles**.

We use **a** before words starting with a consonant:

a jungle   a truck

We use **an** before words starting with a vowel:

an orange   an egg

GRAMMAR Focus

In your book, write *a* or *an* before each of
these words.

1    2    3    4

___ elephant   ___ bush   ___ apple   ___ snake

5    6    7    8

___ caravan   ___ omelette   ___ insect   ___ cabbage

Write the ten words from this box that you would use with **an**.

oak	cap	sun	eel	rug
rat	egg	table	card	ear
inch	box	owl	ant	log
oar	arm	fox	ash	mat

GRAMMAR *Extension*

A Copy these sentences.
Write *a* or *an* in the gaps to finish the sentences.

1 You will find _____ entrance at the back of the building.

2 We had _____ argument yesterday.

3 There are thirteen in _____ baker's dozen.

We use **an** before a silent 'h':
   It would be **an** honour to be made team captain.
We use **a** before 'u' and 'eu' when the sound is 'y', as in 'yes':
   A metre is **a** unit of measurement.

B Write *a* or *an* before each of these words.

1 uniform   2 house   3 hour

4 umbrella   5 unicorn   6 hotel

Check-up 2

Verbs

Write the **verb** from each sentence.

1 The curtains hang over the windows.
2 The bird is pecking at the ground.
3 I work hard at school.
4 They are waiting for the train.
5 I am talking to my friend.

Adjectives

A Write the **comparatives** of these **adjectives**.

| 1 sick | 2 short | 3 smooth |
| 4 plain | 5 small | 6 green |

B Write the **superlatives** of these **adjectives**.

| 1 sad | 2 smart | 3 flat |
| 4 blunt | 5 weak | 6 long |

C Use these **adjectives** in sentences of your own.

1 happy 2 louder 3 easiest

Contractions

Write the **contractions** for these words.

| 1 she is | 2 we are | 3 it is |
| 4 they are | 5 I am | 6 you are |

Adverbs

A Sort these **adverbs** into **how**, **when** and **where** adverbs.

before unhappily often
far nowhere high
untidily soon quickly

B Make these sentences more interesting by adding **adverbs**.

1 The sun shone.

2 The bird flew.

3 We ran in the race.

4 They swam in the river.

Prepositions

A Write all the **prepositions** you can find in this story.

The fox ran behind the dustbin and jumped on the fence. It leaped into the tree and ran along a branch. It jumped down and disappeared through the hedge. The fox looked around, slipped inside a shed and hid between some old boxes.

B Use these **prepositions** in sentences of your own.

1 over   2 between   3 away

Articles

Write *a* or *an* before each of these words.

1 arm   2 city   3 umbrella

4 bag   5 house   6 uniform

7 aeroplane   8 bicycle   9 unicorn

10 shop   11 hour   12 oven

Verbs

Verbs are doing or active words.

When we use verbs to tell us about something that is happening now, we use the **present tense**.

> The frog **jumps** into the pond.
>
> or
>
> The frog **is jumping** into the pond.

When we use verbs to tell us about something that happened in the past, we use the **past tense**.

> The frog **jumped** into the pond.

To make the past tense, we usually add 'ed' to the verb family name.

If the verb family name ends in 'e', we just add 'd'.

The snowball roll**ed** down the hill.   The girl smile**d**.

Copy the sentences below into your book.
Underline the **past tense verbs**.

1 We wanted to go out on Saturday.

2 We voted to go ice skating.

3 We skated all afternoon.

4 I needed a rest when we got home.

Find the verb.
Think of its family
name, then add
'ed' or 'd'.

Copy the sentences below.
Change the present tense verbs to the **past tense**.

1 Ronan and Clive talk to each other on the telephone.

2 The children cook pizza for tea.

3 I decide which book to read.

4 The boys laugh at the joke.

5 They smile and wave at their friend.

GRAMMAR *Extension*

Copy this table.
Fill in the missing words.

Verb family name	Present tense	Past tense
to chew	she _____ he is _____	they chewed
to watch	we watch they _____ _____	I _____
to _____	I paint he _____ painting	we _____
to finish	you _____ you _____ _____	you _____
to _____	they ask I am _____	he _____

Confusing words

We sometimes confuse words because they have similar spellings and sounds.

These three words can get mixed up:

where   **were**   **we're**

It is quite easy to tell the difference.

We use **where** when talking about a place:

> **Where** are you going?

We use **were** when talking about something that happened in the past:

> They **were** setting off yesterday.

We use **we're** as a contraction for 'we are':

> **We're** not allowed on the school field if it is muddy.

Two other words that can be confusing are **there** and **their**.

There usually means a place:

> The cinema is over **there**.

Their means 'belonging to them'. It is about people:

> They made **their** coats dirty.

Look for the smaller word 'here' in **there**. 'Here' also means 'a place'.

'I' is in the middle of **their**. 'I' is also to do with people.

GRAMMAR *Focus*

Copy the sentences below into your book.
Choose the right word to finish each sentence.

1 Where/Were are you going?

2 If were/we're late we won't get in.

3 I think we catch the bus over there/their

4 Where/We're did you find there/their hats?

A Copy these sentences.
Choose *where*, *were* or *we're* to fill the gaps.

1 Many people ____ queuing to see the match.

2 "____ almost there," said Dad.

3 "____ do we go when we get inside?" I asked.

B Copy these sentences, choosing *there* or *their* to fill in the gaps.

1 Max went to his friends' house and played with ____ dog.

2 They had a picnic for ____ tea.

3 "I like to go ____ ," said Max.

GRAMMAR *Extension*

Look back at Unit 3 to remind you about 'two', 'too', and 'to'.

Choose the correct words to finish these sentences.

1 There / Their is nothing left to / two eat.

2 Tell me we're / where I can go too / to buy some food.

3 The best place to / two go is over there / their

37

Singular and plural

Singular means 'one thing or person'.
Plural means 'more than one thing or person'.

If we are talking about more than one thing we usually add 's' to a noun. This makes it plural.

one eagle   two eagle s

Some nouns need 'es' on the end to make them plural. These nouns end in:

ch   sh   s   x

Singular	Plural
stit ch	stitch es
wi sh	wish es
bu s	bus es
gla ss	glass es
bo x	box es

Nouns ending in 'zz' need 'es' to make them plural. There are very few nouns that end in 'zz'.

GRAMMAR *Focus*

A Make these singular nouns **plural**.
Write the plural nouns in your book.

1 dish   2 trench   3 punch

4 grass   5 fox   6 cross

7 ditch   8 rash   9 gas

10 march   11 gash   12 finch

B Use five of your **plural nouns** from part A in sentences of your own.

Be careful! Some of these nouns may only need 's'.

Copy these tables.
Fill in the missing words.

Singular	Plural
bush	
arch	
	gashes
tree	
	witches
tax	
church	
coach	

Singular	Plural
	compasses
mass	
table	
pitch	
	guesses
torch	
	carts

GRAMMAR *Extension*

Write the words ending in 'es' which match these descriptions.

1 We use these to tell the time.   w _ _ _ _ es

2 These books contain maps of countries.   a _ _ _ _ es

3 Places where you make sand castles by the sea.   b _ _ _ _ es

4 These are areas of swampy ground.   m _ _ _ _ es

5 Girls sometimes wear these.   d _ _ _ _ es

6 the daughters of a king and queen   p _ _ _ _ _ _ es

Adverbs

An **adverb** tells us more about how, when or where the action of a verb takes place.

How: The lightning flashed **brightly**.
When: The thunder rumbled **later**.
Where: The rain fell **here**.

Adverbs are sometimes used in pairs to make the meaning clearer.

I walked **more slowly** than my friend.

These adverbs can also tell us more about other adverbs:

quite	only	so	almost
very	rather	less	most

GRAMMAR *Focus*

Write in your book the pair of **adverbs** from each sentence.

1 The cat crept rather slowly towards the bird.

2 The bird went on quite happily pulling a worm from the ground.

3 Very quietly, the cat crept closer.

4 Almost silently, the cat jumped towards the bird.

5 The bird flew very quickly into a tree.

Grammar Practice

Choose a different **adverb** to improve the meaning of each sentence.
Use adverbs from the box if you wish.

more
very
so
rather
less
extremely

1 Put away the glasses _____ carefully.

2 You need to paint _____ colourfully.

3 When we move away, we will visit _____ often.

4 The train is running _____ late.

Grammar Extension

Find the verbs, then put an adverb or a pair of adverbs with each verb.

Improve this story by adding at least six **adverbs** or **pairs of adverbs**.

Night fell and the wood became dark and gloomy. The two friends rode along and talked. They heard rustling in the trees and stopped their horses. One of the men got off his horse and listened. There it was again. "What shall we do?" whispered the man on the horse. "I don't know," the other replied. "I think we should ride on and get out of this wood."

UNIT 18

Verbs

To put a verb in the **past tense**, we usually add 'd' or 'ed' to the verb family name.

Verb family name	Past tense
to look	look**ed**
to argue	argue**d**

Some verbs do not follow this rule.
The verb 'to be' is one of them.
Here is the past tense of the verb 'to be'.

It is useful to learn the past tense of the verb 'to be'.

Singular	Plural
I was	we were
you were	you were
he was	they were
she was	
it was	

Sometimes, we need to change the middle vowel sound to make the past tense.

Present tense	sing	write
Past tense	sang	wrote

GRAMMAR *Focus*

Match the **present tense verbs** in one box with the correct **past tense verbs** in the other box.
Write the pairs in your book.

| grow make hike |
| come throw jump |
| hold bake draw |
| play give shine pile |

| threw drew held grew |
| played gave baked |
| came piled hiked |
| shone jumped made |

Copy the sentences below.
Change the verb in brackets to the **past tense**.

1 We (arrive) at school early this morning.

2 The teacher (give) us some jobs to do.

3 I (mix) the paints.

4 My friend (clean) the paintbrushes.

GRAMMAR *Extension*

Some verbs do not seem to follow any rules to help you make the past tense. For example, the past tense of the verb 'to go' is 'went'.

A Write the **past tense** of these verbs. Use a dictionary to help you.

1 to go	2 to leave	3 to speak
4 to catch	5 to find	6 to have
7 to meet	8 to eat	9 to sleep

B Copy the sentences below.
Choose the correct verb to put the sentences into the **past tense**.

1 I am/was cross with Judy.

2 The day was/is cold and damp.

3 The children ran/run across the field.

4 Butter is make/made from milk.

Sentences

Every **sentence** must make sense.
There are three things a sentence needs to help it make sense:

| **a capital letter** | | **a full stop** |

The eagle **flew** over the mountain.

a verb

 GRAMMAR Focus

Copy these sentences into your book.
Give each sentence a **capital letter** and a **full stop** and underline the **verb**.

1 the wind blew around the house

2 my family lives in the country

3 i am sitting in my chair

4 we are going on holiday

5 the stone cracked the window

6 the boy tripped on the step

7 the gate creaked in the wind

8 they are playing in the field

Be careful! Some of the sentences have two verbs working together.

Practice

is

looks

was painted

am looking

used

Choose a **verb** from the box to make each of these into a sensible **sentence**.

1 I _____ _____ at the picture.

2 It _____ very beautiful.

3 The picture _____ very old.

4 It _____ _____ a long time ago.

5 The artist _____ lots of colours.

Extension

Past tense verbs can be one or two words.

A Add a **past tense verb** to complete each **sentence**.

1 Louis _____ into the house.

2 He _____ _____ by the thunder.

3 The rain _____ quickly.

4 The lightning _____ across the sky.

5 Louis _____ under the bedclothes.

B Use each of these **verbs** in a sentence of your own. Remember the **capital letters** and **full stops**.

1 am flying

2 were sitting

3 closed

4 dug

5 was running

6 is making

Check-up 3

Proper nouns

Copy these sentences.
Write the **proper nouns** with a **capital letter**.

1 cardiff is the capital of wales.

2 new year's day is hot in australia.

3 The river thames runs through london.

Adjectives

A Read the passage right through then write it out adding **adjectives** to fill the gaps.

The _____ house stood by the side of the _____ road. There was a _____ garden at the front and the back. The garage was painted _____ and _____. _____ trees grew around the house making it _____ and _____.

B Make the adjectives in brackets into **comparative adjectives**.

1 That piece of cake is (small) than this one.

2 There is a (long) piece of string in the drawer.

3 The river by the other bank is (deep).

C Make the adjectives in brackets into **superlative adjectives**.

1 This is the (high) of all the hills.
2 This is the (proud) moment of my life.
3 Use the (clean) cloth you can find.

Confusing words

Choose the correct words to complete the passage.

In too/two days time were/we're going to/too visit our cousins. There/Their house is in the country and we're/where taking a taxi from the station. Were/Where they live is very beautiful because their/there is a river and a lake two/too.

Verbs

A Change these sentences from the present tense to the **past tense**.

1 We swim in the sea.
2 I run for the bus.
3 The cows chew the grass.

B Change these sentences from the past tense to the **present tense**.

1 Many people played golf.
2 The children sang every morning.
3 The elephants liked the water.

C Choose the right word to finish each sentence.

1 The plants *is/are* growing well.

2 I *am/is* writing a letter.

3 We *was/were* allowed to go outside.

Contractions

Put the apostrophe in the correct place in these **contractions**.

1 Im   2 youre   3 hes   4 shes

5 its   6 were   7 theyre   8 dont

Adverbs

Copy these sentences and add **adverbs** to fill the gaps.

1 The clowns juggled _____.

2 The ringmaster cracked his whip _____.

3 The crowd clapped _____ _____.

Prepositions

Use these **prepositions** in sentences of your own.

1 between   2 over   3 through

4 in   5 under   6 near

Articles

Write *a* or *an* before each word.

1 bush   2 antelope   3 hour

4 umpire   5 hero   6 island

7 donkey   8 uniform